Embroidery Design Profits

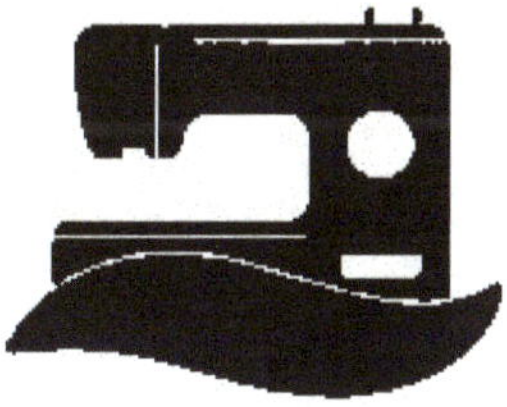

By TREV HUNT

ISBN:
ISBN-13:

DEDICATION

This book is dedicated to you, the reader. I hope you find it insightful & interesting enough to take the plunge into the world of Embroidery.

CONTENTS

ACKNOWLEDGMENTS

I'd like to thank everyone I've worked with over the years. Designers, digitizers, suppliers & the very many customers from around the world.

1
LET'S BEGIN

Welcome to the second book in this series. The first book contained a lot of information about me and how I got into the embroidery business, so please consider reading 'Embroidery Machine Profits' if you haven't already. I must assume that many of you will already have read that book, so I don't think it's necessary to include all of that same information again in this one.

In this book I will concentrate on just Embroidery designs and I'll show you the many different ways you can make money out of them.

When starting into any new venture, it always helps to have some knowledge of the industry you intend to operate in. Readers of the first book will already know about all of the video tutorials available on my Youtube channel 'Embrocraft', so please also have a look at them sometime after you've read this book.

I've also just released three other books to complement the first two. They are 'The Embrocraft A to Z of Embroidery, 'The Embrocraft A to Z of Sewing', and 'The Embrocraft A to Z of Fabric'. All three books are intended to be an A to Z of the terms used in those particular areas, along with explanations of the meanings etc. If you are new to the world of sewing & embroidery, they simply offer a quick reference guide to the many unusual and quirky terms used in the industry. Kindle subscribers may be able to access those books through the Kindle lending library at no cost. You'll find more info on them in the useful links section of this book.

Before we delve into the main subject matter of this book, I'd first like you to take a moment to ponder what brought you here in the first place.

It's quite obvious that you're reading this because you're interested in starting a new business, but what's not always obvious, is why some businesses are infinitely better than others, by a country mile. This book may be about 'Embroidery Design Profits', but it will also offer an insight into 'other things'. Some of those things you may already know, but experience tells me that no matter how many times we are told something, it can still take an awfully long time to sink in.

An unfortunate consequence of living in the western world, is the constant need for money to survive. Everything costs money, so your ability or inability to earn it, can have a dramatic effect on your lifestyle. I do firmly believe that anyone can improve their earning potential, provided they take the time to properly understand even just some of the methods at play in various types of businesses, and how you can use them to generate an income.

We are repeatedly told by parents and teachers throughout childhood about the importance of getting an education, it's instilled in us from an early age.

Once I completed my education/indoctrination, I quickly learned that schools, colleges and universities, were created with an ulterior motive, which is to provide institutions and industries with cheap labour. There is always an easy way and a difficult way to do anything, so although the education system in your country will teach you many things, when it comes to making money, they always appear somewhat reluctant to teach you any alternative to the difficult route. In their minds, there often is no alternative to being a wage slave.

For this reason very few people will start successful businesses straight out of school. It takes time to transform yourself from wage slave to business owner.

There are book snobs in them there hills, and I'm referring to those people who say 'I refuse to read any book that has an 'Introduction'. – I don't wish to offend anyone, so this first chapter was intended only to serve as a brief 'segway' into the second, but to avoid the wrath of those who refuse to read such things, it was not an introduction, I've tried my best to avoid one of those.

Now we move swiftly on to the next chapter.

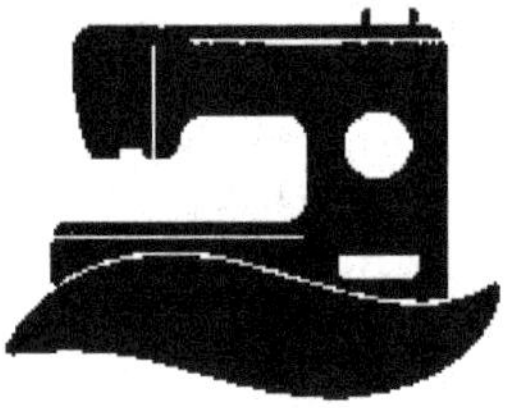

2
A DIRTY LITTLE SECRET

In this chapter we're going to have a look at different business models.

Most first businesses are either sales businesses or service businesses and both types have their limitations. Sales businesses usually involve buying in products and selling them on for a profit, typically twice what you paid for them. Buy for $1, sell for $2 etc. If you get more sales, then you need to buy in more products and keep stock etc. If you have even a reasonable level of success, before you know it you'll need storage and an office, and that costs money. You may be selling those products for $2 each, but you only made $1, less any selling expenses. Then your government will expect a cut of every sale. All those little things add up to a big chunk of every sale that is not yours, and when you eventually sit down to do the real math's, you'll quickly realize that you're actually making very little money.

You'll convince yourself that the only way to improve the situation is to get more sales, then get bigger premises and maybe even hire some staff. If you ever make it that far, those extra costs will have to come out of that already tiny slither of profit on each sale. Then further down the line you'll sit down again and realize that you're still not making any money and the problems are getting worse.

The real issue lurking in the background is that most people fool themselves into believing they can fix things just by getting more sales, and you can't, not unless you're selling many thousands of higher profit items, which is unlikely to happen. Not only that, but you'll need a strong flow of regular sales just to stay afloat and will never be very far away from bankruptcy. The only way it has a chance of being successful, is if either your profit margins are freakishly high, or you're making the products yourself etc.

The dream is real enough, but you will only get so far because the reality of that business model sucks. Businesses like Ebay still try to sell that dream, but as most of you will have already discovered by now, the reality of selling via that platform is somewhat different in practice. Sales businesses are not as easy as they first appear. Selling can be hard, and having to work for every sale can be a serious challenge in itself.

Service based businesses are another common

startup, Gardening, Landscaping, Painting & Decorating, Plumbing, Web Design, Computer Repairs, Consultant etc. Many of these opportunities for self-employment will last much longer than any sales business, but for the most part, your earnings are limited almost exclusively by how many hours you can work in any given week.

Gardening is one of the worst businesses, because depending on where you live in the world, you will lose many hours, days, weeks and months to bad weather and varying daylight etc. The profits can be quite acceptable in some of these tradesman type businesses, but the big drawback, is the need to continue working every day or the money stops. Once you add a few household bills into the mix like rent, mortgage, car payments etc, you can quickly become a slave to it. You're now tied to that business and can't stop even if you wanted to. Once you've been trapped in that situation for a while, you will eventually grow to resent it (just as I did).

Having realized the limitation of their selling skills and the reality that most service businesses operated by individuals are governed by the hours you can work, The next level of business might be a hire businesses or something similar. This type of business can take many forms, but generally manifests as a bouncy castle hire, tool hire. This business type is an improvement over previous areas mentioned as your equipment can be in many different places at the same, in place of yourself. Thus gaining the ability to make a lot more money than is possible by just the sweat of your own labour.

Cleaning services can also be profitable in large cities, where customers are charged a high hourly rate, staff are paid a low hourly rate, and the business skims the difference. Other people are out there making money for you. This is a good admin style middleman business.

Now things start to get interesting. We're going to look at a different class of products, some are digital, some are physical, but all share the same common trait.

Here's a short list:
Feature Films
Songs/Music Tracks
Software Products
Embroidery Designs
Paperback Books
Ebooks

Video Training
Stock Photography
Stock Video
Photoshop Actionscripts

The list could easily be much longer, as it can include almost anything that can be sold as a downloadable. The common trait that all of these products share is that you only need to make them once, then you get to sell them over and over again, for many years into the future. Some have a lifecycle of 5 years, others can last for 20 years or more. In the case of books, I recently came across one little known author who is still making money from a book he wrote in 1985, that's 35 years ago!

Some real magic can happen for those who continuously produce products of this type, you will quickly start to benefit from the snowball effect it creates. Every product of this type created by you will be sent out into the world to make you money. You should view every one of them as a digital soldier with a mandate to make you money. Some will inevitably do better than others, but the more products you create, the more digital soldiers will be out there working for you. Do that for a year or two and the full force of the snowball effect will eventually kick in. Unlike a conventional business that stops when you stop, with a digital business, if you need a break and can't or don't want to work for a while, the money will continue to flow anyway, for many years to come.

One noteworthy point to take from this is that a high proportion of the world's most successful businesses operate in the realms of Software, Movies, Publishing & Digital Media. They all share that same trait of making a digital product once, then selling it many times over.

Digital Products

This nudges us gently onward to the subject of this book, Embroidery designs. It is very much a similar type of product to those previously mentioned, it's just easier to produce an embroidery design vs making a movie, writing a book, or creating a software program.

3
BIG FAT PROFIT MARGINS

Embroidery designs are an essential ingredient for any embroidery business, but they can also be used as the foundation for a very profitable standalone business. There are three main ways to make money with embroidery designs.

1) Create designs & make products yourself.
This particular subject was covered in great detail in my first book 'Embroidery Machine Profits'. The products you make can be anything from simple embroidered patches to a range of embroidered products or your own clothing

brand. There is also many opportunities to create a unique clothing business targeted at specific sporting goods markets, like fishing, motorsports, golf, rugby, football etc. It is only limited by your imagination.

2) Offer an embroidery digitizing service.
This one is reserved only for the more experienced digitizers. It takes a special 'skill set' to digitize for custom work, so it's one to put on the backburner for now. Although, it is always possible to outsource projects to a much cheaper overseas based digitizer and skim the price difference (I've done it many times!).

3) Create stock designs & resell the files.
This is the realm we are targeting within the scope of this book and there are a few ways to get started.

Learn to digitize your own designs.
There are plenty of free online tutorials for specific embroidery digitizing software programs.

It's really about whether you have to the time or the inclination to learn how to digitize. But once mastered, you are free to create as many designs as you wish at no further cost. This is obviously the best option, but embroidery digitizing is not an easy skill to learn. The cost of digitizing software can be prohibitively expensive, then it will still take time to get to grips with. If you wish to get a business up and running quickly, you will most likely need faster options.

Outsource your digitizing projects.
This is the route most people take. You simply find yourself a reasonably priced digitizing service, agree prices and start sending them projects. Using services of this type is significantly cheaper if you can supply them with a vector graphic of your design. Projects sent without a vector graphic will often incur a small artwork charge.

There are tutorials available on how to turn a simple jpeg into a vector graphic using a program like adobe illustrator. It's much easier than you think and learning this quick skill will save you a lot of money. Embroidery digitizers work purely online these days, so they are often based overseas in various locations. There is nothing wrong with finding a service in your own country, building a working relationship and only using them, these people are normally highly skilled individuals who know their trade inside out. But that experience frequently comes at a premium price. You can expect to pay up to $25 to get a design digitized by an expert based in the USA or UK, but it's pretty easy to find someone based in China or India to do the same project for $5 to $12 per design.

You might be shocked already at how quickly the

cost of these services could rack up if you want a bunch of designs produced, but all of these services usually offer a substantial discount for bulk digitizing projects. The way to get those costs down is to test them out with an individual project, then get a price for 50 projects at once.

In the past I've been able to get a full set of 250+ world flag designs digitized for just $750 all in, they were digitized for just $3 each. I now have 9 different sets of world flag designs. When you get them made that cheap, you're in profit with just one sale. It's just one of the ways I built up a large range of designs in a fairly short time period. Not only have I used them to make thousands of flag patches over the years, but as I own those designs, I can now also sell the embroidery files. They can pay for themselves very quickly indeed.

Auto-digitizing.

This option is something to consider as a half-way house method, but it is not a magic wizard that produces perfect results. Designs created in this way will usually need some fettling to bring them up to an acceptable standard. For this reason 'auto-digitizing' is often frowned upon, it is seen as a 'low quality' option, but if you were to learn some basic digitizing skills and combine them with auto-digitizing, it's entirely possible to make some sellable designs. The concept here is to use the auto-digitizing function of a software program like PE-design or Wilcom Hatch, to create the basis of your design, then you make manual adjustments to improve the quality & finish of the design. I will explain a quick method of doing this in a later chapter.

Buy in a range of designs to resell.

Most embroidery businesses will jealously guard their embroidery design library, they frequently do not ever resell their designs. Those that do will sell their designs under a license agreement. That license will limit the buyer to using the design to only make products, but you cannot resell the design file itself. That's a sensible system for any purveyor of embroidery designs, you do need to stop people from just doing whatever they like. Another method employed to limit reselling capability, is to only supply the design in one particular embroidery format. That way it becomes a real pain for anyone wishing to resell, as they'd need to create all of the other design formats for that design. That's not so easy to do from a random embroidery format. Most outsourced embroidery projects will include an embroidery file of the .EMB or EMT type when you get them back from the digitizer. These are the source files generated by whichever Wilcom Software program was used by that particular professional digitizing service. Design files supplied in other formats will have a limited capability for resizing or making adjustments, but if you have the native/source embroidery file, you can do quite a bit more with them. Even a simple program like the free version of Wilcom Truesizer will let you resize & reshape a design to an acceptable standard.

Virtually none of the existing stock design suppliers online will allow you to resell their designs, they also won't sell their designs in bulk. In those rare cases when they do, they will retain some protection by not giving you the source file.

The solution is to create your own versions of popular designs and do the same thing as the big boys and retain the source files. It's always going to be better to have your own collection of products to sell, that way you'll receive very little flack from other sellers.

Making money from embroidery designs.
Regardless of whether you create your own, outsource the creation, buy them in to resell, or even combine all three options to expedite your launch, you will want to know how much money

you could reasonable expect to make. So for arguments sake we'll assume that you did just that, combined the options, some were cheap, some were free, and some you paid over the odds to have digitized elsewhere. The average cost worked out to be $5 per design.

Here's the numbers based on selling each design individually on your own website or a site like Etsy. Now keep in mind that the lifecycle of a new design is at least 25 years, so we're looking at this as 'the potential number of sales over a 25 year period'.

1 sale = $ 5
2 sales = $10
3 sales = $15
4 sales = $20
5 sales = $25
6 sales = $30
7 sales = $35
8 sales = $40

9 sales = $45
10 sales = $50
15 sales = $75
20 sales = $100
25 sales = $125
30 sales = $150
35 sales = $175
40 sales = $200
45 sales = $225
50 sales = $250
60 sales = $300
70 sales = $350
80 sales = $400
90 sales = $450
100 sales = $500
150 sales = $750
200 sales = $1000
250 sales = $1250
300 sales = $1500
400 sales = $2000
500 sales = $2500
600 sales = $3000
700 sales = $3500
800 sales = $4000
900 sales = $4500
1000 sales = $5000

All of this sales potential for an outlay of just $5. If those numbers seem excessive, I'm going to show you another way to look at this, as it will blow your mind wide open to the potential.

1 sale in 5 years for 25 years = 5x$5=$25
1 sale in a year for 25 years = 25x$5=$75
1 sale in 6 months for 25 years = 50x$5=$150
1 sale in 3 months for 25 years =100x$5=$500
1 sale per month for 25 years = 300x$5=$1500
2 sales per month for 25 years = 600x$5=$3000
1 sale per week for 25 years = 1300x$5=$6500
2 sales per week for 25 years = 2600x$5=$13000
3 sales per week for 25 years = 3900x$5=$19500
4 sales per week for 25 years = 5200x$5=$26000
5 sales per week for 25 years = 6500x$5=$32500
6 sales per week for 25 years = 7800x$5=$39000
1 sale per day for 25 years = 9131x$5=$45655
2 sales per day for 25 years = 18262x$5=$91310

I did warn you that digital products can be seriously profitable! – Now obviously some designs are more popular than others, some will rarely get a sale, and others will sell several downloads per day. Designs often go through phases of popularity, it can simply depend of whatever is popular at the time. You can compensate for this with the addition of a range of seasonal designs. Valentine's day, Easter, Halloween, Thanksgiving, Christmas etc. Birthday & pet designs are popular all year round.

Micro-investing.

If you were to look at those numbers again from a viewpoint of 'micro-investments', the potential return from embroidery designs is ridiculous. If you created them yourself, or they were sourced for less than $5, you're in profit with the first sale.

Another way to boost your sales is to create themed design sets. You simply take 5 to 10 similar designs and sell them as a discounted set. If you've outsourced the creation of that set, then it may take longer to get your money back, but sets do have a tendency to sell faster than individual designs. You're also getting $25+ per sale, not $5. This represents good value to many potential customers, so they'll frequently choose to buy a set if it appears to be better value. Having said that, do not dismiss selling designs individually, as some buyers are always low-balling, looking for the cheapest option to get what they want, and they are the very folk who buy designs individually. Much depends on where and how you sell them. It's just a matter of trial & error to find out which options your customers appear to favor on that particular sales venue and how much they are willing to pay.

4
EMBROIDERY MACHINES & FILE FORMATS

Embroidery Machines can be broadly placed into three categories. Domestic, semi-commercial, and commercial machines. File formats used for most domestic and semi-commercial machines will contain color information for that particular design. The file formats used for most commercial machines do not carry color information, instead, the colors are programmed into the machine for each design.

Embroidery file formats broadly fall in to two categories. The first, source formats, are specific to the software used to create the design. For these formats, the digitizer keeps the original file for the purposes of editing. The second type, machine formats, are specific to a particular brand or model of embroidery machine, they contain primarily stitch data (offsets) and machine functions (stitch, trims, jumps, etc.) and are thus not easily scaled or edited without extensive manual work.

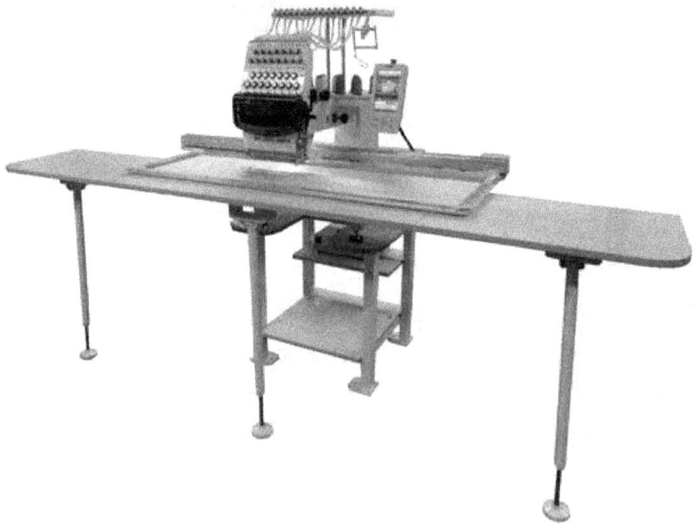

However, because these files are easy to decode, they serve as easy exchange formats, with some formats such as Tajima's .dst and Melco's .exp being so prevalent that they have effectively become industry standards and are often supported directly by machines built by rival companies, or through provided software to convert them for the machine.

Many machine embroiderers use conversion programs to convert from one machine's format file to another, with varying degrees of reliability.

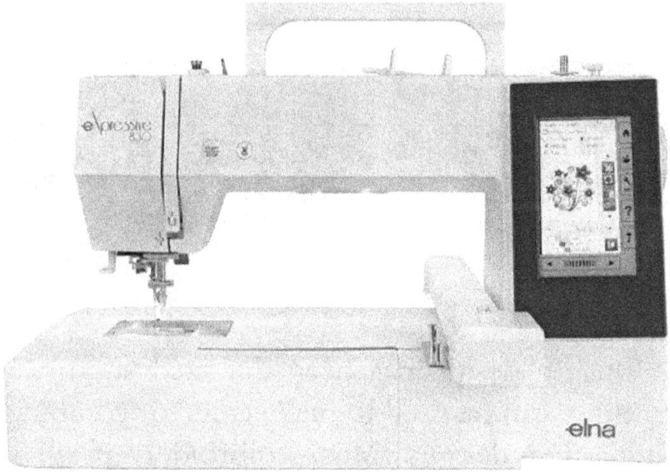

A person who creates a design is known as an embroidery digitizer or puncher. A digitizer uses software to create an object-based embroidery design, which can be easily reshaped and edited. These files retain important information such as object outlines, thread colours, and original artwork used to punch the designs. When the file is converted to a stitch file, it loses much of this information, rendering editing difficult or impossible.

Editing embroidery designs

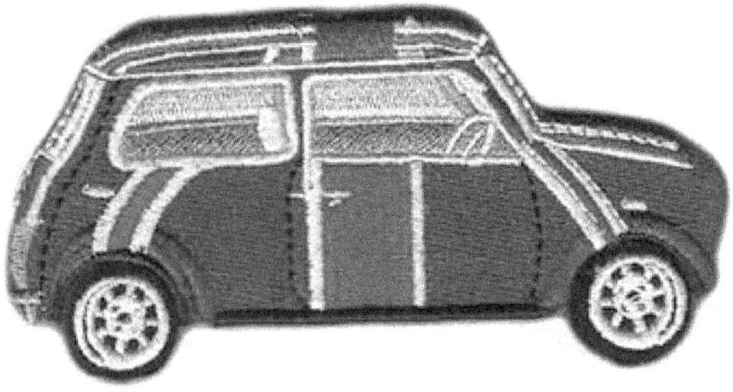

Once a design has been digitized, a software program can be used to make edits, or combine it with other designs. Most embroidery programs allow the user to rotate, scale, move, stretch, distort, split, crop, or duplicate the design in an endless pattern. Most digitizing software programs allow the user to add text quickly and easily, or change the colours of the design. More sophisticated packages allow the user to edit, add, or remove individual stitches. Most modern embroidery machines have fairly simple built-in design editing features.

Loading a design into the machine

After editing the final design, the file is loaded into the embroidery machine. Different machines require different formats that are proprietary to that company. Embroidery patterns are normally transferred to modern embroidery machines via a USB flash drive, although other methods of file transfer do still exist.

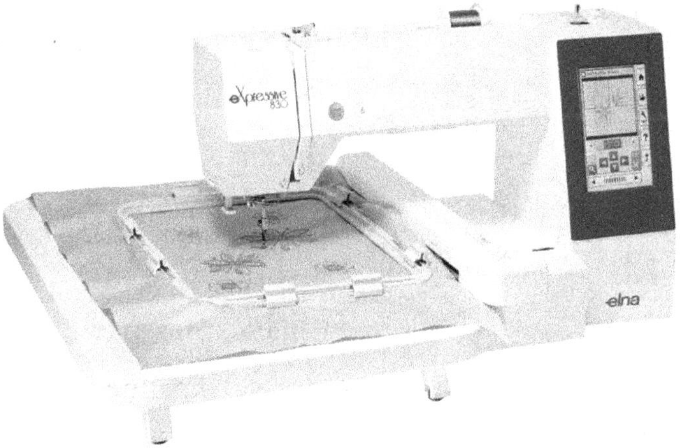

Embroidery File Types

File Type/Extension	Company/Machine compatibility
10o	Toyota

File Type/Extension	**Company/Machine compatibility**
ART	Bernina Artista
ASD	Melco
CND	Melco Condensed
CSD	POEM, Singer EU, Viking Huskygram
CXM	Proel TSI, Millennium X
DAT	Barudan FMC
DST	Tajima, Brother, Barudan, Babylock, Melco, Richpeace
DSB	Tajima Barudan
DSZ	Tajima ZSK
E?? (?? = 01-99)	Barudan Tajima
EDD	Richpeace
EMD	Elna Expressive
EXP	Melco Expanded, Bernina
F?? (?? = 01-99)	Barudan ZSK
FDR	Barudan FDR
FHE	Singer (Futura)
FMC	Barudan FMC
GNC	Great Notions Condensed

File Type/Extension	Company/Machine compatibility
HUS	Viking Husqvarna
JEF/JEF+	Janome, New Home
KSM	Pfaff
M3	Juki B
OEF	OESD Condensed
OFM	Melco
PCD, PCS, PCQ	Pfaff
PEC, PEL, PEM, PES	Baby Lock, Bernina Deco, Brother, Simplicity, Melco
PHB, PHC	Baby Lock, Bernina Deco, Brother
PMU	Proel, ProWin (Proel TSI)
PUM	Proel, ProFlex (Proel TSI)
RPF	Richpeace Welcome
SEW	Elna, Janome, New Home, Kenmore
SHV	Viking Husqvarna
SST	Sunstar
STI	Toyota/Data Stitch
STX	Toyota/Data Stitch

File Type/Extension	**Company/Machine compatibility**
TAP	Happy (HappyJapan)
TBF, TCF	Tajima
U?? (?? = 01-99)	Barudan
VIP	VIP Customizing
VP3	Pfaff, Husqvarna Viking
XXX	Singer, Compucon
Z?? (?? = 00-99)	ZSK

(The following paragraph is a shameless plug!) Many designs from my own collection are sold via the Embrocraft shop on Etsy.com. The products are mainly geared towards the production of embroidered patches and I've put many of them into themed packages or collections. It serves as an example of a thriving little embroidery design shop. I only built that particular shop in June 2020 and it's already doing very well.

5
CREATING YOUR OWN DESIGNS

Every new embroidery design starts with a source image. Whatever method you utilize to obtain that image is really up to you. Some people just search google images for design ideas, others buy image collections from design sites like Envatomarket.com. Another option is to create them yourself. If you're familiar with with programs like Adobe Illustrator & Photoshop, then it's quite possible for you to create a design image from scratch, then save it as a vector image.

Software programs created for the specific purpose of embroidery digitizing, always work best with vector graphics. So if your design image is a .jpeg or .png type image, you'll need to convert it to either an SVG, AI or EPS format for best results.

A quick way to do that:

1) Open adobe illustrator
2) Drop the image into the program

3) Highlight the image and choose the 'Trace Outline' option. (there is a 'tracing workspace' option in the latest versions of illustrator cc.)
4) Start the tracing process.
5) Once completed, save/export as SVG file.
6) Drop SVG file into Brother PE-Design (use 'import vector' option).
7) Image will auto-digitize without selecting any options. (other image types may not auto-start).

Digitizing programs like Brother's PE-Design, will let you drop in a jpeg or png with the option to auto-digitize it, but most often it does a poor job with those image types. But drop in a vector graphic in SVG format, and it will automatically start the digitizing process and will do a far better job of it. Much depends on the clarity of the image and how complicated the design is. The quality of the images used, will have a big impact on the output of the software. Simpler designs auto-digitized in this way will often come out close to perfect every time. I say close, because there can be minor irritations like unwanted gaps between elements etc. You may wish to change the stitch type of some elements, for better visual effect, and understanding stitch density will help prevent thread & needle breaks for the end users of your designs.

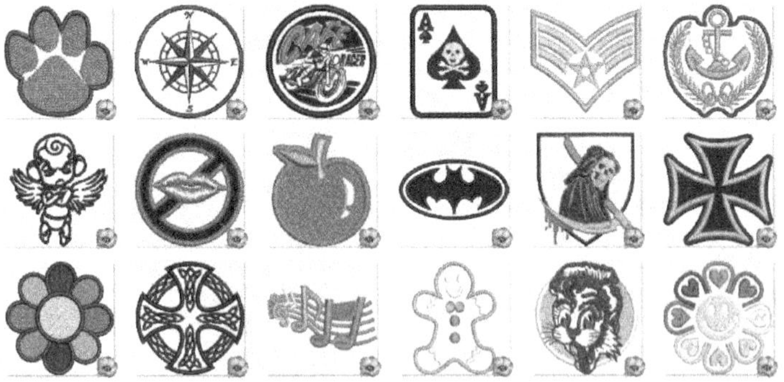

There are also many other options to aid the creation process. I currently use a program called 'Logomaker'. It has a huge collection of templates and resources built-in, with options to obtain extra design packs for future upgrades. It contains literally thousands of shapes, objects and symbols, every one of them can be resized, warped, skewed, duplicated etc, with a full colour palette available for every individual element. It's a wonderful bit of software. I know there's a lot of people making money creating logo's with that program, they sell their logo creation services via Fiverr.com. That is an optional sideline business in itself, and one to keep in mind for future reference. My goal is to help you get a business up and running, by whatever means, so I'm throwing as many bones at you, as I can muster.

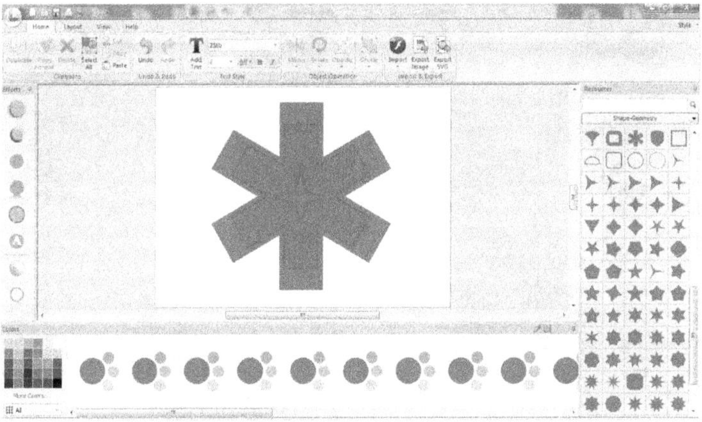

This Logomaker program makes it very easy to create an entire logo from scratch, from simple designs to advanced company logo's. Best of all it can output an SVG vector graphic of any design you create, which can then be dropped into Brother PEDesign for instant digitizing.

The combination of Logomaker and PE-Design is a very slick system for creating embroidery designs from scratch. It is literally all you would ever need. I'm currently talking to them about a potential promotional offer for patrons of the Embrocraft youtube channel, as I write this, so once that is sorted, I will place relevant links in relevant video descriptions on that channel and in the back of this book if it's sorted out before I publish.

It's also possible to outsource the creation of the vector graphics your embroidery designs will be based on, but I'm fairly sure that will prove to be a very expensive way to get things done. It's much cheaper to buy a collection of images and then either digitize them yourself, or send them out for bulk digitizing at a discount.

6
EMBROIDERY DIGITIZING SOFTWARE

There are quite a few different embroidery digitizing programs out there, and in the past I've played around with lots of them. It's only fair to say that most of them have a difficult learning curve, they are just not that easy to use. That would also have to include Wilcom's digitizing software. The recent introduction of their Hatch digitizing software was a welcome alternative to their ridiculously expensive commercial software (up to a whopping $10k). The full Hatch program costs $1000, and it's still far from easy to use. That's why my own default software is Brother

PE Design, and yes they too have a version that costs $1000, the all you really need is the entry level program at $400. PE-Design appears to have the opposite problem to most digitizing programs, it makes it look too easy. At first glance it can fool you into thinking that you can't do very much with it, but you'd be wrong. Most of the same features available in Hatch, are also present in PE-Design, but for reasons best known on to the creators of Brother PE-Design, you really do have to dig for them. It's almost like they are trying really hard not to scare you away.

The result of all of that is a really useful chunk of software that just works right out of the box. They have made it very easy for even a complete newcomer to grasp. There are also a ton of free video tutorials on Youtube, that will help you learn very quickly how to use PE-Design. Even though I've been familiar with the software for years, I still occasionally find a feature that has been in every version and I didn't know it existed. It's that kind of program, it has hidden depths, but in a good way. Like all embroidery software you will still need a powerful computer to run it on, or you'll suffer some serious lag while making even simple edits. At the very least I'd advise you to upgrade the memory on your pc to a minimum of 8gb if it's still running on an older type spinning hard drive, replace it with an SSD (solid state hard drive). Those simple upgrades will make a world of difference to the time it takes to make edits or digitize on an older computer. Regarding computers, if you want a fluid digitizing experience, I'd recommend a newer Intel i5 or i7, or alternatively, a 2nd or 3rd generation Ryzen 5 or 7 will be sufficient. Digitizing software is resource hungry, so you really need a fast and powerful beast, with similar specs to a modern gaming pc.

It's also good to know that Brother makes it remarkably easy to create a design in PE-Design and load it straight into a Brother embroidery machine. That function can prove pretty handy for testing out new designs.

7
EMBROIDERY SOFTWARE TRAINING

As previously mentioned, you can't really do better than the mountain of free tutorials available on Youtube. It's possible to find tutorials on just about any aspect of any software program, it's never more than a quick search away. For anything else you simply refer to the manual. Brother PE-Design comes with an enormous manual in PDF format, which details every feature in the program and how to use it. That's something we all tend to avoid like the plague, but sometimes it really is easier to just read the manual. Larger software vendors like

Wilcom, do provide real training courses that you can sign up for and attend at various locations, I could almost guarantee there will be one available in your country, several times per year, just don't expect it to be either cheap or easy.

If you hope to make a living out of something, then it stands to reason that you might be willing to invest the time and money in some real training from one of the big software vendors, it certainly won't hurt. Any principles learned can also be adapted to other software programs when needed.

I should remind you of the other option available to you, and that is to not bother learning to digitize at all. You can choose to outsource all your projects or buy in everything, then use a free program like Wilcom Truesizer to resize designs and change formats. That way you don't even need to buy expensive digitizing software, and can spend that money on getting embroidery files to resell.

You will always have the option to do as little or as much of the process as you like. If you are purely only interested in getting other people to make the designs and you just sell them, you can cut out much of the process. But that does not mean you should avoid taking the time to understand the processes involved. Customers will ask you questions and you'd better have the answers. Equally there is always a temptation to buy or download collections of embroidery files from Ebay and similar places, those 80k embroidery file collections etc., that I've mentioned previously. What you probably don't know is that apart from them being a living nightmare to navigate through, all of those design files belong to companies like Disney, Brother, Janome, Husqvarna etc. If you are silly enough to attempt to sell them, they will come after you with a vengeance, so please don't make that mistake.

Copyright infringement is a big deal these days and a criminal offence in many legal jurisdictions, which would include the UK & the USA who are fully prepared to throw your ass in jail over such matters. As most of the readers of this book will be from one of those two locations, and I've already shown you many ways to create or source your own products, I'd advise you to not mess with the big boys.

8
OUTSOURCING YOUR DIGITIZING PROJECTS

You can find digitizing service providers in many ways. In the past I've even found them through spam in my junk email folder. There is no shortage of them. Most google searches will help you find digitizers online in the country you live in, but they are nearly always the most expensive people to use. If you want to find someone for a more reasonable price, then you need to dig a little deeper. I have used quite a few different services over the years, but I found them all in the same two places, Ebay & Fiverr.com.

The service providers that advertise on Ebay, did appear to possess the ability to create designs to a much higher standard than any of the services I have ever used via the Fiverr website. That's probably because the feedback & seller rating systems on Ebay do severely penalize sellers who don't make the grade. I have to admit that it does a good job of sorting the 'wheat from the chaff'. Fiverr on the other hand is unfortunately full of 'have a go heroes', who have a tendency to write checks that their bodies can't cash. Only 1 in 4 digitizing services I tried on Fiverr could produce a design to an acceptable standard.

The thing to remember is that once you find a good digitizing service via one of those platforms, you should start communicating with them directly by email outside of that platform. The platforms in question may have policies that prohibit such behavior, but I don't have any such policy, so stuff them. It's better for both of you to be outside of those platforms in the long term, it will make your workflow smoother. Many digitizing services will offer a monthly account for regular users, so you will simply get a bill for completed projects at the end of each month. That can be handy enough if you wish to pay them out of money generated from sales. It can also make it easier to budget for new projects.

Building up a long term business relationship with your digitizer, can often pay dividends. Many of these services are often run by just one self employed person trying to make a living, just like you are, and when you start dealing with them on a regular basis, they can become friends. Over time your new friend will start doing you little favors here and there, which can lead to getting work done both cheaply and for free. It's just one of the benefits of sticking with the same service provider for a few years. Keep that in mind, as that friendly digitizer can save you a small fortune over time.

Next we'll look at testing your embroidery files.

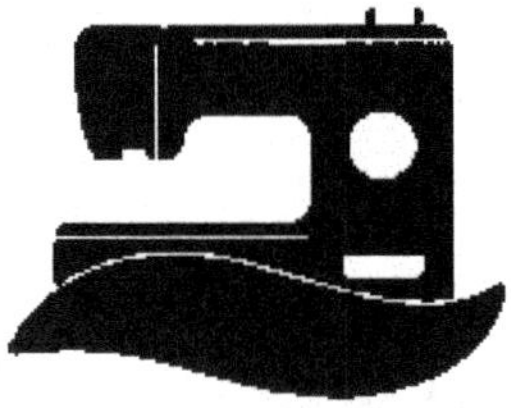

9
TESTING NEW DESIGNS

Although it's not strictly a necessary part of the process, there are three main ways to test your embroidery files.

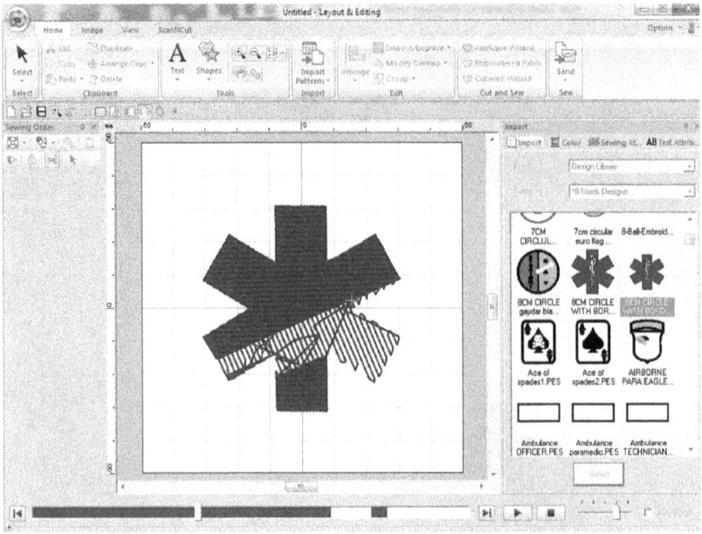

1) A simulated stitch-out (see previous image) within your embroidery software program. This can really only show you where stops, link stitches and colour changes will occur, but may also show up some glaring flaws, if they exist.

2) Ask your digitizing service to do a test stitch-

out (as shown in the previous image). Many digitizers will offer this service at a small cost, or sometimes at no extra cost. They will test the design on a real embroidery machine and send you a picture of the final stitched out design.

3) Buy a cheap embroidery machine. Even a used example of a Brother PE770E/F440E or similar would be perfect for design testing purposes. Used examples of these can be purchased on Ebay for as little as $300.

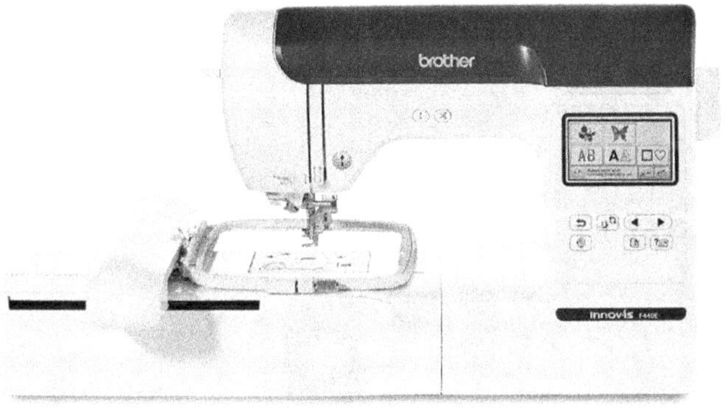

When you start creating your own designs from scratch, it's always nice to see exactly how they will stitch out. It creates opportunities to fix designs and learn how to make minor adjustments to things like stitch density etc, then view those changes in real life.

You can learn a lot from this process, it also allows you to find and fix any design flaws your customers may inform you about. If you've read my first book 'Embroidery Machine Profits', you'll know just how useful an embroidery machine can be. Who doesn't like multiple streams of income.

10
PREPARING DESIGN FILES FOR RESALE

Once you have obtained some embroidery designs to resell, you will need to get them ready. This seemingly simple process can quickly become complicated if you don't plan ahead. It's quite common for embroidery designs to be made available in various machine formats, it's also common for some vendors to offer up several size variants of a design. Sounds simple enough? Until you realize that if you offer 10 embroidery formats and 5 sizes, you'll be creating more than 50 files for each design. If that seems like too much trouble, then it pays to know that most embroidery designs are around 3 inches (7.5cm) in size, so if in doubt, just create one version at 3 inches, and let the customer resize the design if needed. This will simplify the creation process for you and take much less time to create those zip files ready for download.

You will typically create one download folder for each design. That folder should contain the following items: Embroidery files, Preview Image, Production Worksheet PDF. Some sellers also include an embroidery file viewer and pdf viewer, but these are optional.

Here's how you can create these items.

Search for and download the following programs:
Wilcom Truesizer, the free version works fine.
7-Zip (it's free).
Screenhunter, or any other free screenshot program).
PDF Printer Software, MS office has this feature built in, otherwise, search for 'CutePDF' as it is freeware.

First create a main project folder for the design.

Then use Wilcom Truesizer to convert the design into as many formats as you wish to create, you

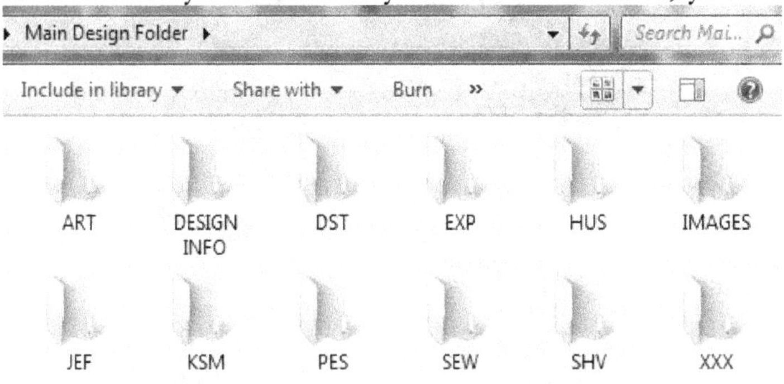

can only make them into one format at a time, and you'll typically create 10 formats. You will also need to create 10 sub folders, then place each file format into the relevant folder. This would usually be .DST, .PES, .HUS, .JEF, .ART, .SEW, .XXX, .EXP, .KSM, .SHV file versions, so give your 10 folders the same 10 format labels.

While Truesizer is still open, find the design properties tab and choose print worksheet option (you may need to select your PDF printer software as the printing device, then save to desktop). Your PDF document should print and appear on your desktop. Create another folder labelled 'Design Info' and insert PDF.

With the design still showing in Truesizer, take a design screenshot. It has two uses, one for your listing image and the other as a customer preview within the download folder. The default grey background in Truesizer, can be changed to other colours like white etc. Place that screenshot/preview into a new sub folder marked 'Images'

Close the main project folder, then right click it to reveal the menu, then choose 7-Zip from the dropdown list and .zip as the archive type. Save newly create zip file to desktop. Other archive formats like .rar are available, but most users either won't understand them or won't have the software to unzip them. Windows can unzip standard zip files, 7-zip simply does it a better job of it. Stick with .zip files and you won't go far wrong. Do not password protect your zip files, your customers will hate you for it.

That's really all you need to do to create a sellable embroidery file, just remember to keep a copy of the screenshot preview for the sales image. Also remember to back up everything and store that backup somewhere safe. Hard drives fail, folders can get accidentally deleted. Backups are a lifesaver.

If you wish to scale things up and create hundreds or thousands of sellable downloads at once, there are a few essential software programs you can buy to help speed things up.

Adobe Photoshop

Most of you may already have this, but may not have made use of its action record function or batch processing option. When faced with the prospect of editing/processing hundreds or even thousands of images, there are ways to speed things up.

For example: Let's say you need to resize a batch of 500 images to 1200 pixels wide, so they all uniformly fit the requirements for your etsy shop etc. Here's how it's done in all recent versions of photoshop:

Step 1: Open your folder of images and drop the first image into Photoshop, select 'Window' from top bar menu, then choose 'Actions' (or press Alt F9).

Step 2: In Actions window select small tab in the top right hand corner to open more options, then choose 'New Action'.

Step 3: Name the Action (name it something like 'resize1000wide'). Then hit the record button.

Step 4: Choose the 'image' tab from the top bar menu, then select 'image size' from the dropdown sub-menu.

Step 5: Set the image size option to 1000 pixels wide, then hit ok.

Step 6: Choose Ctrl S (file save), then Ctrl W (file close), then go back to the actions window and click the 'Stop' icon to stop recording.

Step 7: From top menu in Photoshop choose File/Automate/Batch. Then choose the source folder for your 500 images. You will find that the action script you just recorded will already be chosen in that batch option screen.

Step 8: Click OK to start processing the images. Images will flash quickly in your open photoshop screen as they are processed. On most modern computers the entire batch will be resized in minutes.

That was just a very simple example of what you can do with batch processing in Photoshop. It's possible to record far more complicated actions, then apply them to a batch of 10,000 images if desired.

Converting Batches Of Embroidery Files

If you were to create a large collection of designs, then converting them into various formats can quickly become a very time consuming project. There are many programs out there that profess to offer batch conversion options, (Wilcom Hatch has this function built in) but after trying many of them, I can only recommend one in particular.

Data7 Conversion Tool:
This batch embroidery file converter can convert a folder containing thousands of embroidery designs into most other embroidery formats. There are 25 different formats to choose from,

but it can only convert into one format at a time. This handy software program costs just USD$31, and as I write this, it's currently on offer for just USD$8. I have no affiliation with them, it's just a handy tool to have. Their website is Data7consultancy.com. Once you've converted your designs into various formats, you'll find yourself with a collection of designs in many formats, that all need to be sorted out into the correct folders. This can appear to be a complete nightmare if you are unprepared, but there is an easy way and a difficult way to approach any task. I'm going to show you how to make it really easy for yourself and this solution will help to turn you into a very productive individual from this day forward.

Organizing Your Design Catalogue

Let's say for example that you've created 1000 Embroidery designs and need to convert them and then organize them into sub folders, then finally zip them up into a download package.

Organizing 1000 designs will require you to perform the following tasks.

Step 1: Create 1000 folders up to 15 sub folders.
Step 2: Create up to 15 sub-folders for every design.

Step 3: Insert a design image into the relevant sub-folder for each design.
Step 4: Insert a pdf of the design specification sheet into the relevant sub-folder for each design.
Step 5: Insert any customer instructions into the relevant sub-folder for each design.
Step 6: Insert each file format into the relevant sub-folder for each design.
Step 7: Create a zip file of each design folder.

At some point in this process you will inevitably feel the need to rename your designs, or even design folders. Many digital plaforms cannot handle long file names, so it's often easier to rename your designs with an SKU type system. The easiest way I've found to create unique SKU's is 2 letters +4 numbers +1 letter (ED1234D etc.), If you were to attempt this renaming task manually on a large batch of files, it will take forever, but as a veteran of these tasks I've found a bit of free software that does it all quickly. You can download it directly from them at **advancedrenamer.com.**

Advanced Renamer
This program has many smart options, like find/replace, renaming the folders, or renaming just the files in the folders. It also many other

features like adding incrementing letters or numbers, or both together, even 'in reverse order' etc. I've found it to be a huge time saver over the years and you can't beat a freebie.

Now we need to get back to the subject of organizing all of those folders and yet another handy little software program to make life easier.

My first introduction into anything even resembling a computer, was a manual typewriter – wow! Then I graduated to an electric typewriter – double wow! Eventually I took the plunge and bought my first real x86 computer which ran Windows 3.0 (that's the version before Windows 95) hell yeah! – All I ever used it for at that time was writing letters and printing them off. More recently I quite often find that people are still doing little more than browsing the web and printing off letters. It's very easy to be fooled into thinking that your computer is only slightly more useful than your television, but you'd be very wrong.

Any modern computer is only as good as the software installed on it. When bought from new they usually arrive packed full of trial software that amounts to sod-all. An office suite and Photoshop can add some usefulness, but most often people just browse the web and buy stuff. The real revelation of the power of computing only became apparent when I started using Macro's in my workflow.

The most recent macro program I'm using is a little program called Remouse. It's comes in 'free' and 'paid for' varieties, but once you've tried it you will really, really want it. It is by far the most useful program any digital product monkey can ever install on their PC, and although the free version can be manipulated to become useful, the full unrestricted version is worth every penny of their $25 asking price.

Remouse:
It is essentially a simple mouse recorder program that can be utilized in many ways to complete repetitive tasks, (like taking thousands of files and sorting them into the relevant folders). Similar to a Photoshop action script, you just record yourself doing a task once, then set it to repeat the actions you just did over and over again. Except that those tasks can be very complicated and unique. Here's a simple example:

You could record yourself dropping an image into Photoshop, then play a photoshop action script, then move the completed file into another folder, then zip the folder up. – In the past I've even used this program to created hundreds of website listings. Any repeatable task or command can be automated at up to 10x human speed. It becomes especially useful when you realize that it does not need to rest, go to the toilet or take tea breaks, it just gets on with it like a relentless Duracell bunny. In 2015 I was asked to help someone (paid help!) with a monster of a project that he estimated would take his office of 10 people, two years to complete. It involved the creation of multiple versions of a range of digital products. There would only actually be 500 sellable products at the end, but a total of 150,000 files needed to be created from scratch, using Illustrator, Photoshop, Corel Design and MS Office. Once created they all needed to be organized into sub-folders and eventually download zips.

The Solution: I set up 5 of his office computers to run re-mouse and the relevant software package, he then ran them 24 hours per day at 3x human speed for 4 weeks. It didn't even interfere with his other projects, it just silently ran in the background while his staff worked on other things on other computers. I only spent one day there and showed them how to automate it all. We even had it dropping completed files onto a network drive, to be picked up by the next computer in a continuous workflow.

That's the sort of work that computers were designed to do, most people have not one clue just how productive we humans armed with computers can be, we just need to try a little harder and think outside the box. That guy was fully prepared to pay 10 people's wages for 2 years to get his products made, but by pure luck, in a chance conversation, I told him that most or all of his project could most likely be structured into repeatable tasks and then automated. I sincerely hope that after reading this, you will utilize Re-mouse, or a similar program (I have no affiliation with any of them) and think of new ways to tackle monster projects.

11
HOW TO SELL

If you were to scour the internet for Embroidery stock design businesses, you will discover that some truly enormous online shops already exist for stock embroidery designs, many of them have been around for years. But therein lies their problem. Many of those shops were built in the late 90's, or early 2000's, they are old and clunky, many have not been updated for quite some time. The internet has been through many changes in recent years, and any website that wishes to be indexed by Google in 2020, must be built on HTTPS for greater security. Websites that don't follow this new standard are being fazed out of search results, it's one of the tools Google are using to clean up the web and make it a safer place. Older websites and online stores that were built using a mindset that's 20 years behind the times, are rapidly disappearing from search results, and rightly so.

Once upon a time, the accepted web development plan was 'bigger is better' when it came to building shops on the web. That lead directly to some enormous embroidery design shops being built with 50,000+ individual listings etc. The problem with that is the same issue you'll quickly discover if you were ever to foolishly buy one of those Embroidery design DVD's frequently sold on Ebay, the one's that boast 80,000 designs etc., that I mentioned in a previous chapter. You can't possibly even view that many designs in a reasonable timeframe, never mind actually do anything with them. If you were to view 100 listings per day, it would still take you 500 days to see everything.

Modern online shops now create their listings in a different way. If you have 1000 products to sell, it no longer makes sense to have 1000 individual product listings, instead the accepted method is now to have 100 listings, then each listing has 10 variation or options etc. This makes for a cleaner website and it's easier for people to view your range of products in less time. This is one of the main reasons we create design sets or packages.

If you find yourself with an abnormally large number of embroidery files, then you probably need to sort them into sets and sell them in that way, otherwise people will quickly lose interest if they can't find something they like within a reasonable amount of browsing time.

Design Media & Delivery Methods:

CD Rom's

Although now viewed as a medium of the past, there are a surprising amount of genuine embroidery file sets still being sold on Amazon on Cd Rom format. People do appear to still buy them, but as I don't expect there'll be too many CD/DVD Rom's fitted to the computers of the future, I can't recommend trying this approach in 2020.

USB Flash Drives

Popular and convenient for many reasons, but sending items by post can bring its own problems. If you sell to customers in other countries, they may have to pay extra import duty & taxes on the products you sold them, and they won't be too happy about it (I'm referring to my own past experiences of selling in this way).

Digital Downloads

This just seems to be the best all round solution for 2020. Minimum maintenance, instant delivery & no postage costs, this is as close to an automated money making system as you will get. What's not to like? The most difficult decision you will face is whether to build your own download shop or sell through a third party venue. Both methods have their advantages, so it's down to your own personal choice. You can always choose to do both.

12
SUMMARY

It has occurred to me that this book would not be complete unless I stress to you the need to keep pushing forward with a business of this type. Making a collection of designs, sticking them online, then sitting back and waiting for the money to flow, will only get you so far. If you are starting from scratch as a seller on any sales platform, it will take some time to get established on that platform. There are many reasons for that, but trust and exposure can play a big part in any apparent lack of interest in your products.

Some platforms intentionally limit the flow of traffic to new sellers, until they are more established in that community. Google does the exact same thing with new websites and online shops. You will most often get just a small trickle of free traffic for the first 3 months, then it will increase a little and stay at that new level for another 3 months. Then at around the 6 to 9 month mark, they remove you from the sandbox and it just takes off like a rocket.

In an earlier chapter I mentioned the snowball effect that can happen when you sell digital products online. Businesses of this nature have a tendency to start off slow, and those first six to nine months can be painfully slow, but if you keep churning out new products and keep the faith, eventually it will start to gain traction and produce some real money. When you get to that stage of things, don't forget to regularly pump a little money back into creating more designs, as the longer you do it, the more designs you'll have and the bigger that snowball will get.

Once you have a few thousand designs behind you, it all becomes much easier, as you will always have designs that are trending. There are fast selling and slow selling items in any sales business, but they all play their part in building up your business. It can be tempting to cut out the non-performing designs after a few months of no sales, but that is often a big mistake, as they all have the potential to make money, they're just waiting for their turn to come around. That can be a problem if you're selling on a third party platform and have to pay listing fees, but it won't be a problem if you've thrown caution to the wind, unleashed the hounds and built your own online shop! - Nothing feels better than not having to answer to Ebay/Amazon/Etsy etc. Building your own digital download shop means that you make the rules and you reap the rewards.

There are many options available to expedite the building of an online shop. Here's a quick list from the top of my head.

1) Etsy
2) Shopify
3) Bigcommerce
4) Wix.com
5) Squarespace

6) Hosted Wordpress
7) Self Hosted Wordpress
8) Easy-Digital-Downloads
9) There are sellers on Fiverr.com, who will build you an online shop in just 24 hours for $50 all in.
10) Freelancer.com, hire one to build a shop.

13
USEFUL LINKS

We've now reached the end of the book. If you enjoyed the ride then please leave a nice review and consider reading my other books which are all available on Amazon.

Thanks for taking an interest in my book.

Trev Hunt.

Useful links:
Embrocraft on Etsy:
https://www.etsy.com/uk/shop/Embrocraft

Embrocraft on Youtube:
https://www.youtube.com/channel/UC7GhMfkdH5WJuGZFCM9FYLQ

Please note the YT channel is a work in progress and may not be completed until summer/autumn 2020.

MORE BOOKS BY TREV HUNT

Embroidery Machine Profits.
Embroidery Design Profits.
The Embrocraft A-Z of Fabric.
The Embrocraft A-Z of Embroidery.
The Embrocraft A-Z of Sewing.

ABOUT THE AUTHOR

Trev Hunt has been working in the Embroidery industry in the UK for many years and has written five books on the sewing and embroidery industry. Now close to retirement, he is sharing his experience with you, in the hope that you too may wish to earn a living in the embroidery sector of the craft industry.